WHAT AM I?

Fast, Strong, and Striped

WHAT AM I?

By Moira Butterfield
Illustrated by Wayne Ford

RSVP

RAINTREE
STECK-VAUGHN
PUBLISHERS
The Steck-Vaughn Company

Austin, Texas

Published by Raintree Steck-Vaughn Publishers, an imprint of Steck-Vaughn Company

Editors: Jilly MacLeod, Kathy DeVico
Project Manager: Joyce Spicer
Electronic Production: Amy Atkinson
Designer: Helen James
Illustrator: Wayne Ford / Wildlife Art Agency

Library of Congress Cataloging-in-Publication Data

Butterfield, Moira, 1961-
     Fast, strong, and striped/by Moira Butterfield; illustrated by Wayne Ford.
          p.   cm. — (What am I?)
     Summary: A riddle asking the reader to guess which animal is being described precedes information about different parts of a tiger's body, how it behaves, and where it lives.
     ISBN 0-8172-4583-9 (hardcover)
     ISBN 0-8172-7229-1 (softcover)
     1. Tigers — Juvenile literature.   [1. Tigers.]
I. Ford, Wayne, ill.   II. Title.   III. Series.
QL737.C23B885   1997
599.74'428 — dc20   96-32110
                                                                    CIP   AC

Printed in Hong Kong.
2 3 4 5 6 7 8 9 0 HK 01 00 99

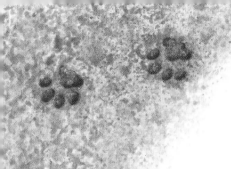

I am furry, big, and strong.

My teeth are sharp.

My tail is long.

My coat is striped.

My eyes are bright.

I am a hunter in the night.

What am I?

Here is my eye.

I see well in the dark, so I hunt at night. Can you see my golden eyes shining in the shadows?

At night, I creep through the trees looking for animals to eat. I can see a wild pig and a deer. Can you?

Here are my teeth.

My teeth are as sharp as kitchen knives. The longest, sharpest teeth are near the front of my mouth. Can you see them?

When I see an animal that looks good to eat, I chase after it and jump onto its back. Then I kill it with my sharp teeth.

Here are my claws.

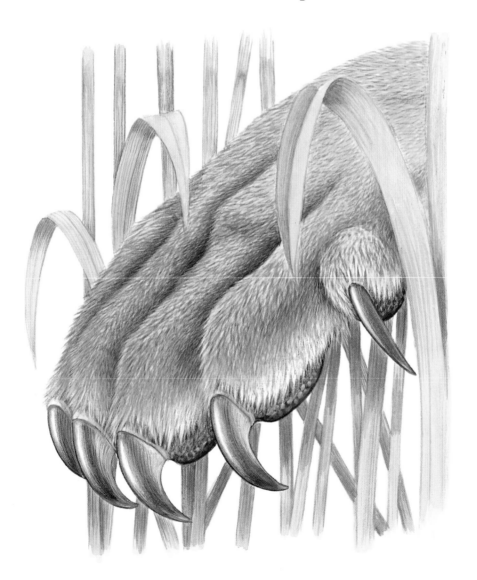

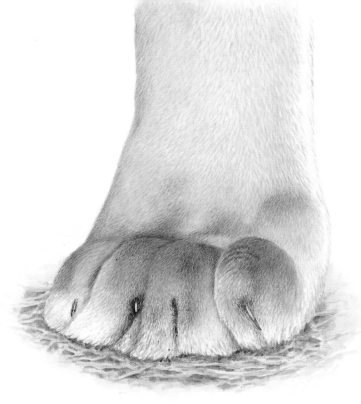

I can hide my claws in my big furry toes or make them pop out. They are as pointed at the ends as needles.

I have four paws. They are soft and padded underneath, like cushions. I walk very, very quietly.

Here is my fur.

It is orange with black stripes. My coloring makes me hard to see when I creep through the bushes.

In the daytime, it is too hot to hunt. I lie down and sleep in the long cool grass, out of the sun's heat.

Here are my ears.

I can hear almost every sound. I can even hear a monkey swinging in the trees above my head.

If the monkey sees me, it will make lots of noise to warn its friends that I am close by.

Here is my tongue.

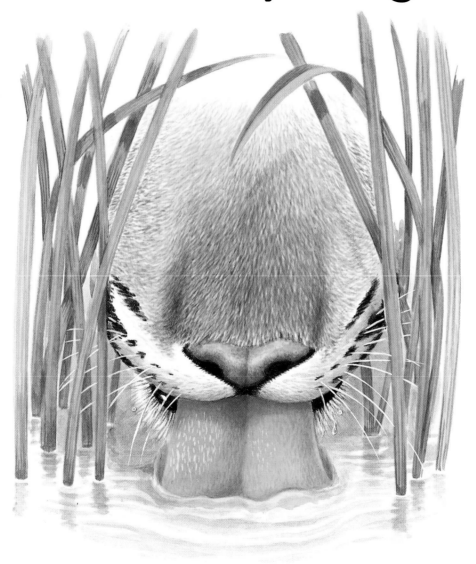

Look how long it is. It feels rough and scratchy. I lick my fur clean with my tongue every day.

I use my tongue to drink from the river. I had better watch out for crocodiles. Can you see any?

Here is my tail.

You can tell when I am angry, because
my tail whips back and forth,
and my long, white whiskers stick up.

Then I open my mouth, and...
roar!
Have you guessed what I am?

I am a tiger.

Point to my…

yellow eyes.

pointed ears.

padded paws.

striped fur.

white whiskers.

long tail.

I am called a
Bengal tiger.

Here are my babies.

They are called cubs, and I am their mother. I will look after my cubs until they are big and strong.

My cubs love to play. This cub is chasing a butterfly. One day my cubs will be able to hunt like I do.

Here is my home.

I live in and around the jungle.

Look for me in the picture. Can you also see two little monkeys, three spotted deer, a snake, and an elephant?

Here is a map of the world.

I live in a hot country called India. Where is it on the map?

Can you point to the place where you live?

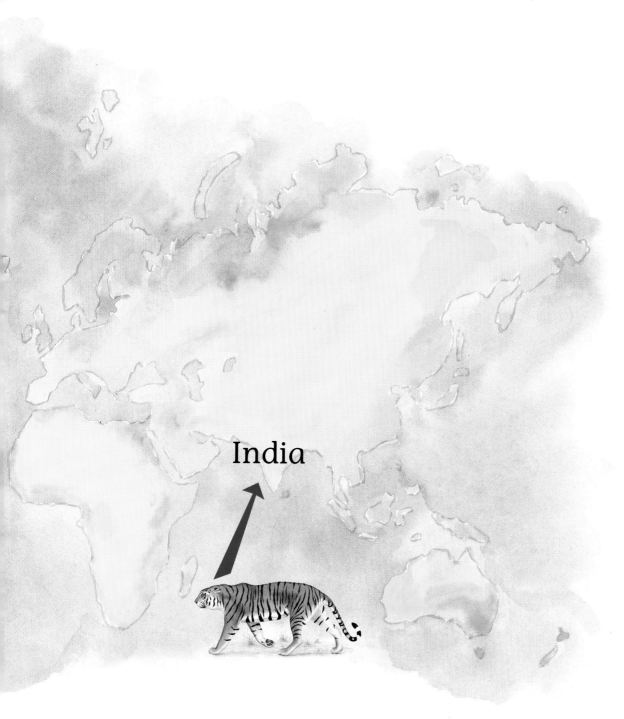

India

Can you answer these questions about me?

How many paws do I have?

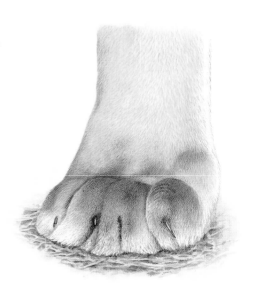

What are my babies called?

Do I like to eat meat?

Do I hunt in the daytime or at night?

What noise do I make when I am angry?

Where do I like to sleep when I am hot?

How sharp are my teeth?

What color is my fur?

Can I see in the dark?

How do I keep my beautiful fur clean?

Here are words to help you learn about me.

claws My sharp pointed nails. They are curved, and they can scratch and tear.

creep This is what I do when I move very quietly and slowly along the ground. I creep when I am hunting.

cub The name for one of my babies.

fur My soft, warm coat. It is orange with black stripes.

roar The loud noise I make. Can you roar like I can?

teeth I use my sharp teeth for biting and chewing. They are much sharper and bigger than your teeth.

tongue I use my tongue for licking and tasting. Mine is much bigger and rougher than yours.

whiskers Fine hairs that sprout from my cheeks. They stick up when I am angry.